Diana

The People's Princess

1961–1997

A Photographic Tribute by **Arthur Edwards**
Written by **Charles Rae** with **Arthur Edwards**
Royal Photographer and Correspondent for ***The Sun***

First Published in 1997 by **News International plc**,
PO Box 495, Virginia Street, London E1 9XY

Written by **Charles Rae** and **Arthur Edwards**

Designed by **Neal Townsend/JMP**

Printed in Great Britain by **Keldia Printing Company Ltd**

The publishers wish to thank all those individuals at
News International who helped in the production of this book

ISBN: **0 9515634 5 9**

Biographies
Arthur Edwards has worked as a *Sun* photographer since 1974. He has been taking
pictures of the royal family since 1977, and of Princess Diana since 1980. He has been
happily married to Ann since 1961 and can't praise her highly enough. They have three
children, John, Paul (who both now work for *The Sun*) and Annmarie.

Charles Rae is married to Jill with two children, Robert and Fiona, and has been a
journalist for more than 30 years. Born in Glasgow, Scotland, he has been a royal
reporter since 1989. He first worked at *The Sun* covering labour news for 10 years
before moving to *Today* newspaper where he began covering the royals.
On its closure he immediately moved back to *The Sun*.

Acknowledgements
The publishers would like to thank the following for permission to reproduce the
photographs used in Chapter One: Press Association pages 8, 11, 12, 13, and Chapter
Nine: Press Association page 125, David Dyson page 124, and Jayne Russell page 119.
With special thanks to Mark Tattersall, Phil Hannaford, Mark Giddings and Terry Richards.

Front cover: Arthur Edwards' last portrait of Diana, Princess of Wales.

Proceeds from the sale of this book will be donated to
The Diana, Princess of Wales Memorial Fund.

1 Virginia Street, London E1 9XP. Telephone: 0171-482 4000. Fax: 0171-782 5605/0171-488 3253

The tragic death of Diana, Princess of Wales turned Britain into a nation of tears and sent a tremor across the whole world.

We lost a woman whose breathtaking compassion highlighted the great unsung causes of our time like Aids and Landmines.

She was a crusader and a fighter, not bothered by convention or protocol.

She was a devoted mother of two boys she worshipped – and for whom she held the highest aspirations.

She was also a stunning young woman whose life was cruelly cut short at a time when she had found happiness.

The Sun's official royal photographer, Arthur Edwards, shared and witnessed many of Diana's magical moments.

This book is an affectionate tribute using Arthur's pictures and written with Charles Rae, *The Sun's* official royal correspondent, to Diana's life and work from the earliest carefree days until the last heartbreaking days.

The Sun wishes to commemorate Diana's charitable works by donating proceeds from this book to the charity founded in her memory: The Diana, Princess of Wales Memorial Fund.

STUART HIGGINS
Editor

Registered Office: News Group Newspapers Ltd., P.O. Box 495, Virginia Street, London E1 9XY.
Registered No. 679215 England

D
Contents

Arthur Edwards Remembers

"I'll tell the jokes, Arthur" **Diana, Princess of Wales**

Diana's romance with Prince Charles was still just a rumour when *The Sun's* royal photographer Arthur Edwards first showed the world the shy teenager who was destined to be Princess of Wales. Cockney Arthur became the Princess's trusted pal as he followed her around the world, capturing the joys and heartache of her royal life. Here he tells of his grief when he heard the news of Diana's death:

"When I first snapped the shy teenager at a polo match in 1980, I could hardly believe she was Prince Charles' new girlfriend. When I went to photograph Diana's coffin being carried out of a Paris hospital, it was the saddest job I've ever had to do. I can't believe I will never take photographs of her again.

"I saw her change from a cheeky, innocent girl into a supremely beautiful woman who was a wonderful ambassador for this country. One of my favourite photos is of young Diana showing her shapely legs in a see-through skirt. I can still see her blushing as I spoke to her about the picture. I will always remember the happy, fun-loving girl of those early years. She loved to laugh and tease me.

"She had the greatest smile of any person in the whole world. As I waited for the coffin to come down the steps, my wife phoned me to ask how I felt. The tears rolled down my cheeks and I had to put the phone down, I was so choked. I had expected to see Diana mature further as a magnificent and glamorous woman. I never thought I would be photographing her coffin. Unbelievably, she will never see her two boys grow up into men. There will not have been many dry eyes in Britain that August day when people heard that Diana was gone.

"Diana left thousands of people feeling better about themselves. That was her magic and the memory I will always carry in my heart. Goodbye, Diana. I'm going to miss you so much."

Diana Princess Of Wales

by Charles Rae

Diana has been injured in a car crash. The news came in a call to my home around midnight on Saturday 30 August 1997, telling me of a car crash in a Paris street. And in the next frantic, shocking few hours I learned the dreadful news that Princess Diana had lost her battle for life. The man she had found happiness with in her last few months, Dodi Fayed, had also been killed, along with the driver of their Mercedes car, Henri Paul. Diana was only 36 but in her short life she became the most famous — and the most loved — person in the world.

In the days that followed the whole world went into mourning. Millions of people in Britain alone grieved for her as if she was a part of their very own family. The vast majority had never met her, but their sense of loss was no less intense than for those who had. Diana touched so many lives, it is hard to imagine how we will all cope without her in the future. She mixed with the rich, but her heart was with the needy. She gave a voice to the silent sufferers. She embraced life with love, laughter and compassion. No cry was too small to be heard and no problem too big to tackle. There are few people who have not been touched by Diana's genuine warmth.

She showed great compassion whether cradling a sick child, comforting sufferers of Aids or Leprosy, or campaigning for victims of landmines. But she also had that sparkle and glamour which endeared her to us even more. From Australia to Zimbabwe, she travelled the world working her special magic. Kings, Queens, Presidents and Prime Ministers all queued up to meet her. But she cut through the red tape of officialdom, determined that her precious time would be spent with the people who had queued for hours to see her. Diana was not only a toucher but in touch with all around her. For a great many disadvantaged people she was their only hope of help — and the image of Diana comforting the terminally ill will be the one that stays in our minds.

Despite her status, Diana was a deeply complex person. She did have a feeling of insecurity and there were bouts of depression and self-doubt, and she battled against an eating disorder. Inside the corridors of Buckingham Palace her hands-on approach was at odds with the stuffy royal courtiers. There were accusations that she damaged the House of Windsor. In reality she dragged it, albeit kicking and screaming, into the 20th century. As a result of her influence, her son William will surely be a popular king when he leads the Monarchy in the 21st century. In fact, Diana did more good than harm to the Monarchy and even when she was stripped of her royal title she immediately got two more accolades from the public that meant even more to her. They dubbed her the 'People's Princess' and 'Queen of Hearts', which is how she herself wanted to be seen. She was the only member of the royal family with whom a whole generation could identify.

Diana was barely 20 when as a shy, naive young girl she joined the most traditional family in the world. Her fairytale marriage to Prince Charles went wrong and there were admitted affairs — he with Camilla Parker Bowles and she with ex-Cavalry officer James Hewitt. But despite all the sorrow and pain in her private life, Diana had found a new tranquillity. She had built bridges with Charles and their two sons, William and Harry, were the most important people in their lives. She and Charles exchanged caring and loving messages right up to her untimely death. The loss felt by Charles, William and Harry is shared by us all. Diana also appeared to have found the one thing she truly craved — happiness. She believed she had at long last found her chance of love with Dodi Fayed, the son of Harrods owner, Mohamed Al Fayed. Without doubt she will be remembered as a humanitarian, and one who swept away taboos with charm and determination. Her battle on behalf of landmine victims took her to Angola and Bosnia. This campaign helped change the minds of the governments that had seemed reluctant to take action until she acted as the victims' standard bearer. Bosnia was her last overseas charity visit, but her three days there did more for the campaign to ban these awful weapons than the many speeches by high-powered international politicians had done.

She was a unique public figure and we are unlikely ever to see her like again. Diana, Princess of Wales lost her battle for life in the early hours of Sunday morning, 31 August 1997 . . . and on that day something inside all of us died as well.

A Life Cut Short

1 July 1961 The Hon Diana Spencer, third daughter of Viscount and Viscountess Althorp born.

1967 Diana's mother, Frances, leaves her husband for wallpaper heir Peter Shand Kydd. Their divorce is one of the most acrimonious in recent history and Frances loses a custody battle for Diana and Charles, her two youngest children.

1970 Diana starts boarding school at Riddlesworth Hall, near Diss, Norfolk.

1974 Diana sent to mother's old school, West Heath, near Sevenoaks, Kent.

1975 Following the death of her grandfather, the 7th Earl Spencer, Diana becomes Lady Diana. She and her father and siblings return to live at Althorp, Northamptonshire.

1976 Earl Spencer remarries, to Raine, Countess of Dartmouth, daughter of romantic novelist, Barbara Cartland.

1977 Diana meets Prince Charles for the first time, at a shoot on the Althorp estate.

1980 Spotted fishing on the River Dee with Charles in Balmoral. Story breaks that she is the new woman in his life.

1981 In February, the Queen and the Duke of Edinburgh announce the engagement of their son Charles, Prince of Wales, to Lady Diana Spencer. Wedding takes place 29 July at St Paul's Cathedral. There is an estimated world television audience of 1,000 million.

1982 Prince William born at St Mary's Hospital, Paddington, London, on 21 July. In November, the first newspaper reports of the Princess's eating disorder, later identified as bulimia, appear.

1984 Prince Harry born on 15 September.

1985 Stories appear in press about Charles' and Diana's marital problems.

1986 Diana faints in public at World Trade Fair in Canada, provoking more public concern.

1987 Diana visits Middlesex Hospital, London. She is photographed shaking hands with Aids-victim, Ivan Cohen, becoming the first high-profile figure to do so publicly.

1988 Diana, president of Barnardo's, makes a heartfelt speech on the importance of a strong family life.

1989 Becomes president of RELATE, and makes speech saying: "Sadly for many, reality fails to live up to expectations."

1990 Diana opens Britain's first counselling centre for women with Aids.

1991 Rumours begin to circulate about Diana's relationship with James Hewitt.

1992 Andrew Morton's book *Diana: Her True Story*, allegedly written with Diana's help and certainly that of her friends, is published in June. It reveals her bulimia, five suicide attempts and that she knew of Charles' affair with Camilla Parker Bowles. In August the "Squidgy" tape is published, giving details of an intimate telephone conversation between Diana and a man later identified as James Gilbey. This leads to much speculation as to who was bugging the Royals. On a four-day trip to Korea, the couple are dubbed 'The Glums'. In December John Major tells the Commons, and Buckingham Palace issues a statement: the Prince and Princess of Wales have decided to separate, but there are no plans for divorce, the split is amicable and their constitutional positions will remain unaffected.

1993 Diana apparently rules out any divorce so she can help groom William to be King and continue to influence her sons' lives. In December Diana announces at a charity lunch that she is withdrawing from public life to find a more meaningful purpose.

1994 In an interview with Jonathan Dimbleby in June, Prince Charles confesses he was unfaithful to Diana, that he was pressured into marrying her and that he never loved her.

1995 In November, Diana appears on the BBC *Panorama* programme. It is broadcast on the occasion of Charles' 47th birthday. In it she admits: being unfaithful with James Hewitt; that she knew Charles was in love with Camilla, and how it devastated her; that she wants to be an ambassador for Britain and to work with the underprivileged; that she believes Charles' friends and staff are against her and will not seek a divorce, to protect her children. In December, Buckingham Palace announces that the Queen requested Charles and Diana to divorce for the sake of their children.

1996 Diana's press adviser Jane Atkinson, issues a statement saying: "The Princess of Wales has agreed to Prince Charles's request for a divorce. The Princess will continue to be involved in all decisions relating to the children and will remain at Kensington Palace with offices at St James's Palace. The Princess of Wales will retain the title and be known as Diana, Princess of Wales." Prince Charles and Diana formally lodge their petition for divorce on 15 July after agreeing terms. The agreement includes: Diana giving up her HRH title at the request of the Queen; an estimated £15 million settlement; having to receive permission to travel abroad except on holidays; adopting the title Diana, Princess of Wales; and, at her own request, giving up her military appointments. Princess Diana severs links with 100 charities in July, feeling they should be free to seek a royal patron. She continues to support Centrepoint, National Aids Trust, Royal Marsden Hospital, English National Ballet, Great Ormond Street Hospital and the Leprosy Mission. On 28 August the divorce becomes final, and the marriage of the Prince and Princess of Wales ends after 15 years. In October, Diana is presented with a humanitarian award from the Pio Manzu Research Centre.

1997 Diana is warned by the Foreign Office not to visit South-East Asia as part of her anti-landmine campaign, as they believe it would be too

dangerous. In April, the Prince and Princess of Wales are reported to be planning joint public engagements following a dramatic improvement in their relationship. In June, an auction of Diana's dresses raises more than £2 million. Lot 79, the blue velvet Victor Edelstein dress Diana wore to dance with John Travolta, is sold for £120,301. Diana announces her plans to continue her campaign to ban landmines with a trip to the former Yugoslavia. In August, Diana is linked with Dodi Fayed, son of Harrods owner, Mohamed Al Fayed. Diana holidays in the Mediterranean with her two boys and Dodi. She is reportedly happier than ever.

31 August 1997 The Princess of Wales and Dodi Fayed are killed in a car accident in Paris. Mr Fayed and the driver are killed instantly when the car hits a tunnel wall at the Pont de l'Alma by the Seine river, near the Champs Elysées. The Princess dies at the Pitié Salpetrière Hospital just after 3am.

Chapter One

The Young Princess

Diana Spencer's proud parents Johnny and Frances Spencer, like other members of the aristocracy, turned to *The Times* to proudly announce the birth of their new daughter. They paid 24 shillings — or £1.20 — to tell the world in 16 words: "On July 1st, 1961 at Park House, Sandringham, to Frances, wife of Viscount Althorp — a daughter." And so Diana Frances Spencer arrived into a world in which she was destined to become one of the most popular and most loved figures of the 20th century — the People's Princess. Her arrival was also to change the royal family forever. Young Diana was brought up a country girl living in the 10-bedroomed home at Park House — the family's rented home on the Queen's Sandringham estate in Norfolk. She adored her baby brother Charles, and close family members saw the first signs of one of the qualities she would become famous for — her deep love of children. She treated Charles — now the present Earl Spencer — like a doll, according to one former nanny, and made him dress up in different outfits.

Diana went to a local nursery school in Kings Lynn. When she was eight years old she was sent to a girl's preparatory school — Riddlesworth Hall in Diss, Norfolk. This period of her life was one of her unhappiest. She was still suffering the emotional turmoil of her parents' 1969 divorce and the ensuing bitter court battle when her beloved father, Earl Spencer, then Viscount Althorp, won custody of his four children: Sarah, Jane, Diana and little Charles. Swimming, ballet and art were her favourite subjects, and already her friends began to notice a sharp wit and wisdom.

Despite her own family problems, Diana's only thought was for fellow pupils who cried themselves to sleep at night. In June 1974 more heartache and a major upheaval came when Diana's grandfather, Earl Spencer, died. That meant her father became the 8th Earl and inherited the vast Althorp House in Northants. Overnight Diana acquired a title that millions would use even after she became a royal Princess — Lady Di! Diana could not bear it when the removal men came to take the family from Norfolk to Althorp. The painfully shy Diana suddenly found herself with a new step-mother when her father remarried in 1976 — Raine, the ex-wife of the Earl of Dartmouth and daughter of the romantic novelist, Barbara Cartland. Diana remained devoted to her own mother Frances and could not accept Raine, and with a child's cruelty Diana dubbed her 'Acid Raine'. Later, Diana and Raine were to heal the rift and became very close friends.

By now sisters Jane and Sarah both had flats in London and in the school holidays Diana would often go to stay with them rather than spend time at Althorp. Ironically, despite her dislike for Raine,

Barbara Cartland was one of her favourite novelists and the bookshelf in her bedroom was packed with her step-grandmother's books. Diana was already like many teenage girls, looking for romance with a handsome Prince.

By now Diana was at another school — West Heath in Sevenoaks in Kent. In the bed next to her in her dormitory was her close friend Carolyn Pride, later Carolyn Bartholemew. She and Carolyn, along with another school chum Victoria Pitman, would later share a London flat together. In 1977 as Diana was sitting her 'O' levels, her sister was introduced to Prince Charles at Ascot. Sarah and Charles got on famously but meanwhile, Diana failed all five of her 'O' levels.

In November that year Sarah invited Charles to Althorp for a shoot and it was there, in a ploughed field at Nobottle Wood, that he first set eyes on the plump teenager who was one day to become his wife. Later he talked to friends about his meeting with the young Diana: "What a very jolly 16 year-old. I mean, great fun, bouncy and full of life and everything."

The following month, Diana left West Heath and enrolled at a Swiss finishing school, the Chateau d'Odex near Gstaad. But Diana did not take to it. After barely two months, and after writing countless letters to her father pleading to come home, she was back in Britain. The only thing she really learned at finishing school was how to ski — a skill which was to become very important in her later royal life.

One of her first jobs on her return was as a nanny to Alexandra, daughter of Major Jeremy Whittaker and his wife Philippa. They lived in a place called the Land of Nod in Hampshire. These were happy times for Diana. She spent three pleasant months looking after the little girl and then she returned to London to sign on to the books of a temp agency called 'Solve Your Problems'. Diana took on jobs which involved cooking, cleaning and washing for many clients who booked her through the agency.

But although her working life was normal she was still the daughter of an aristocrat and still got invited to all the posh parties. In January 1979, aged just 17-and-a-half, Diana was invited to Sandringham for the weekend. Prince Charles was there too. It was the weekend that would change their lives — and their destinies — forever.

These are the pictures I wish I had taken of a very young Diana. But how was I to know that this innocent child would one day become the most photographed woman in the world . . .

I first set eyes on Lady Diana Spencer on 29 July 1980, exactly one year to the day before she walked down the aisle with Prince Charles. But on that first day she was an awkward teenager. I arrived at Cowdray Park polo field in Sussex, following up a tip that Prince Charles was there with a girl called Diana. I remember saying: "He can't be running around with a teenager!" It was only two weeks later, when I saw them together at Balmoral, that I realised the romance was on.

It didn't take long before everyone realised that Diana was more than just a passing fancy for the Prince of Wales, and soon everyone wanted a photograph of her. During this period she was very friendly and didn't let the constant attention phase her at all.

Even when she changed her old-fashioned Renault for a brand new red Mini Metro, it didn't stop the attention. She looked terribly embarrassed one day when she could not get the keys to fit in the lock. Just a few days after these pictures, Diana and Charles announced their engagement and the fairytale was underway . . .

Chapter Two

A Princess Crowned

Diana reached the age of 18 on 1 July 1979, and bought — with proceeds from a hefty trust fund from her father — a £50,000 flat at 60 Coleherne Court in London's upmarket South Kensington. She had enough money to furnish it and to begin buying clothes from the shop that would have such a profound effect on the last few months of her life — Harrods. School pals Carolyn Pride and Virginia Pitman joined her at the flat, along with a skiing friend, Anne Bolton. It was during this time that Diana got her dream job working part-time at the Young England kindergarten in fashionable Pimlico. By this time Charles would phone Diana's flat and the pair would go out to the ballet or the theatre. At the end of her working days with the children, Diana would rush home to her flat to slip on a posh frock, ready to dine out with the Prince of Wales. She would regularly nip to her hairdresser, Kevin Shanley, who had a salon in South Kensington. He was cutting her hair in a particular style at the time, little realising that a million women around the world would eventually copy it and call it simply the "Lady Di" cut.

In August 1979 Diana's heart opened to the Prince as she watched him on TV at the funeral of his beloved uncle, Earl Mountbatten, who was killed by IRA terrorists. They met a short time afterwards at the home of Robert and Phillipa de Pass in Sussex. That evening they sat chatting on a bale of hay. Diana said to him: "My heart bled for you." Charles saw for the first time the compassion that would eventually touch millions of people. Diana told him: "It is wrong that you are lonely, you should be with somebody to look after you."

By now rumours had already started to circulate that Charles had a new girlfriend. *The Sun* Royal photographer Arthur Edwards drove down to Cowdray Park polo field in Sussex after a tip that a girl called Diana was with the Prince. Arthur remembers Diana as an awkward teenager when he first set eyes on her on 29 July 1980: "She was sitting on the seats with ordinary punters. Nothing special, just a pretty teenager. She was chatting away, until she saw my camera — and then posed up for a picture. The 'D' necklace she wore struck me instantly — a real sign of innocence. I couldn't believe that this was Charles' new girlfriend. I remember saying: 'He can't be running around with a teenager!'

"It was only two weeks later, when I saw them together at Balmoral, that I realised the romance was on." Diana was eventually tracked down to her kindergarten and she was asked to come outside to pose for a picture. She agreed, but only if she could pose with some of the children. One of them, three-year-old Scarlett Dyer, is now aged 20. Arthur remembers: "Halfway through the picture session, the sun came out and I saw for the first

time what beautiful legs she had. Later that afternoon, I went back to the nursery and told Diana about the photograph. She blushed, and replied, 'I'd hate to be known as the girl who didn't wear a petticoat'."

The romance was well underway and on 24 February 1981, 19-year-old Diana and the 32-year-old Prince of Wales announced their engagement — and then they had to face the cameras together. When asked if she was in love, Diana blushed and said: "Of course." Charles chipped in: "Whatever 'in love' means..." Just after their engagement was announced, a shy young Lady Di faced her first official function. Ironically, it was a poetry reading by Monaco's Princess Grace — the beautiful fairytale princess who was also tragically killed in a car crash. Charles got out of the car first and told waiting photographers, including Arthur: "Wait until you see this!" Then Diana emerged in a low-cut black Emanuel dress — and she looked simply stunning. Arthur remembers: "It was pouring with rain and Diana was shaking like a leaf with nerves, but the rest of us were simply knocked out by her beauty. We knew then that a new star was about to shine."

The wedding was set for 29 July that year. Diana had just turned 20. When she left the kindergarten that last time, her life was to change for ever. The wedding was one of the most joyous moments in British history. Excitement filled the streets along with laughter, smiles and singing — it was sheer magic. Millions of people packed the route to St Paul's Cathedral — another 500,000 people besieged the gates at Buckingham Palace, and they cheered themselves hoarse when Charles kissed his young bride on the balcony.

Arthur was not prepared for that first sight of Diana in her incredible gown: "It literally took my breath away. I don't think I've ever seen such a beautiful sight. For a second, I was unable to even press the button on my camera." The royal wedding was the most watched event ever on British TV, with some 39 million people tuning in. It was watched in over 200 countries around the world, from New Zealand to New Guinea. Like one of the Barbara Cartland novels Diana had devoured in her early years she believed her fairytale had come true.

After trolling around several nurseries in the west end of London, I finally knocked on the door of the Young England kindergarten in Pimlico and asked: "Does Lady Diana Spencer work here?" I was delighted when Diana agreed to pose for a picture. She insisted on being photographed with two of the children from the nursery. The youngster on the left was three-year-old Scarlett Dyer, who is now a budding young actress.

This happy picture was the first decent photo I took of the couple together. Diana was watching the Prince play polo at Smith's Lawn, Windsor, just before her 20th birthday. She sat down next to Charles on the grass during a break in the game. She turned and gave me such a lovely look of happiness and pure pride. She looked gorgeous — a lady very much in love.

When I saw designer David Emanuel crying at Diana's funeral my mind immediately went back to a rainy night in March 1981 when 'Shy Di' carried out her first official engagement. We knew then that a new star was about to shine.

The day I stumbled across Charles and Diana near St Paul's Cathedral was one of the sweetest of my career. It was two days before the royal wedding, and I was driving past the cathedral on my way to work. I just happened to glance over to the steps and in the corner of my eye, I noticed the Prince of Wales' car. I jumped out, leaving my car on double yellow lines, and rushed over to the church with my camera. The couple emerged literally minutes later, oblivious to anyone or anything around them. After walking a few paces, Diana reached for Charles' hand and he took hers, giving it a loving, reassuring squeeze. It was an extraordinarily tender moment.

On the day of the wedding the late Earl Spencer stood proudly with his daughter on the steps of St Paul's. This was a particularly poignant moment for both of them because the Earl was not in good health. But he still managed to walk his daughter down the aisle — just like any proud father.

To this day, I'll never forget the excitement leading up to the wedding. I remember leaving my hotel in the Strand at 4.30 in the morning, and walking to St Paul's. The streets were lined with people smiling, laughing and singing. The atmosphere was joyous, and I knew it was going to be a magical day. Nothing had prepared me for that first sight of Diana in her incredible gown. And when they left the cathedral as 'Mr and Mrs' they both looked wonderful in the open-topped carriage which took them to begin their honeymoon.

I vow to thee, my country, all earthly things above,
entire and whole and perfect, the service of my love:
the love that asks no question, the love that stands the test,
that lays upon the altar the dearest and the best;
the love that never falters, the love that pays the price,
the love that makes undaunted the final sacrifice.

And there's another country, I've heard of long ago,
most dear to them that love her, most great to them that know;
we may not count her armies, we may not see her King;
her fortress is a faithful heart, her pride is suffering;
and soul by soul and silently her shining bounds increase,
and her ways are ways of gentleness and all her paths are peace.

Thaxted
Gustav Holst (1874-1934)
Cecil Spring-Rice (1859-1918)

Chapter Three

The Princess And Her Princes

Diana made motherhood look so effortless, and despite being insecure about almost everything in her life, it seems she never suffered any doubts about herself as a mother. Where her children were concerned, Diana broke one unspoken royal rule — she was not afraid of showing the public her true affection for her sons, William and Harry.

William was born at 9.30pm on 21 June 1982 and Harry at 4.20pm on 15 September 1984. Despite her two sons being 'the heir and the spare', Diana insisted from very early on that they should not be brought up in the cold, stuffy tradition of other royal children before them. She wanted them to mix with children from all walks of life, and William became the first heir to the throne to be sent to a public kindergarten. But above all, Diana did not want her children deprived of the hugs and kisses she was starved of during her own childhood.

Diana loved her children passionately and was never afraid to say so. On one occasion Diana said: "I always feed my children love and affection — it's so important." Before her divorce she declared: "I will fight for my children on any level in order for them to be happy and have peace of mind and carry out their duties." Her speeches about the importance of hugging children were often seen as a criticism of her husband's upbringing, and of the royal family's carelessness in their treatment of Diana, who herself was little more than a child when she joined them and who, perhaps, suffered from a lack of attention in the early days.

When William was at the crawling stage, Diana and Charles undertook a gruelling four-week tour of Australia. There the Princess broke another royal rule: she was determined to have her son with her — and she won the battle. Diana knew that Charles and the Queen were the only teachers who could pass on the traditions and royal way of life to prepare William for his role as a future Monarch. She was, however, determined that he would be a king who truly knew his people, who knew how they lived and survived in the real world. Diana was not wholly against the country pursuits which her boys, like other members of the royal family, enjoy. But she warned them about being photographed with guns in their hands when she told them: "Remember there is always someone in a high-rise flat who doesn't want you to shoot Bambis."

There were bucket-and-spade holidays for the boys, and outings to McDonald's for hamburgers. She encouraged them to wear jeans and baseball caps, and when they went to the cinema, or to theme parks, she made them queue like everyone else. Diana made them realise that not everyone had enough money to live a privileged lifestyle. Like most mums, she was there for both her sons when they began their first nervous days at school. She was also there at Parents Day, kicking off her shoes, and taking part in the Mother's race —

and winning! Through her sons, Diana was always able to put people at ease. She would walk into a room and tell those she was meeting how difficult it was to get the boys off to school on time — just like any mum! — and immediately those who came into contact with her, whatever their background, shared for a few brief moments, a common problem of bringing up children.

As well as ensuring the children had a normal life, she introduced them into her other life where she went to help those less fortunate. Diana took the boys to meet homeless people and people with Aids. In particular she was teaching William about caring and compassion, to allow him to be a king who truly understood humanity. Diana revealed: "I want them to have an understanding of people's emotions, of people's insecurities, of people's hopes and dreams." Just a few months before she died, Diana told her friend Tina Brown, the British-born *New Yorker* editor: "All my hopes are on William now. I don't want to push him. It is too late for the rest of the family. But William . . . I think he has it. I think he understands."

And baby makes three . . . Everyone assumed the Princess would be in hospital for several days after the birth on 21 June 1982(left). But she surprised everyone when she appeared with William the following afternoon to take 'Baby Wales' home to Kensington Palace. We did not know his name for several weeks and the bookmakers took millions of pounds in what became a national guessing game. Four years later Diana left the same hospital with her newborn son Harry. She looked so glamorous and happy — but it was all a huge act. Her marriage was already falling apart and Charles had rekindled his relationship with Camilla Parker Bowles.

Princess Diana invited me to Kensington Palace in February 1983 to photograph her son William, taking his first steps. Years later I witnessed one of the very last times that Diana attended the traditional family Christmas at Sandringham. She and William chatted happily as they walked to church.

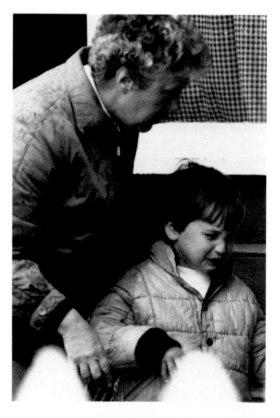

Like most four-year-old boys, William had a naughty streak in him and when he was told he could not do things, he was determined to break the rules . . .

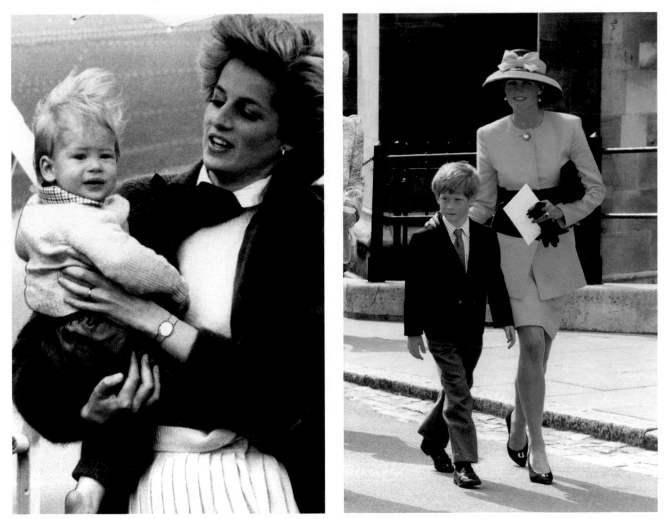

Diana arrived at Aberdeen Airport and it was blowing a gale. She came down the steps of the Royal Flight with Harry, who was barely a year old, looking windswept. But Di still managed to look stunning. She obviously passed on a few sartorial tips to Harry as he smartened up for later public appearances.

. . . William was determined to try to run on to the polo field at Smith's Lawn, Windsor, where Charles was playing, but nanny Olga Powell gave him a stern ticking off and he burst into tears. There was only one person who could console him — his mum, who sat him on her lap and wiped the tears from his eyes. Like magic he stopped crying.

For four or five days we watched as Harry and William learnt to ski on the nursery slopes in Lech, Austria, in March 1991. The big day came when they went skiing with their mum for the first time — sharing a ski lift made for three. Diana had a protective hand on Harry, but she needn't have worried because of the two boys, he has lived up to his daredevil reputation. It wasn't long before Diana was to moan to us: "I just can't keep up with them anymore."

William's first day at Wetherby School in February 1987. Prince Charles claimed he was snowbound at Sandringham, and Diana arrived alone with their four-and-a-half year-old son. Diana was clutching William with both hands, and it was almost as if she was scared to let him go.

In June 1991, I covered Harry's sports day at Richmond Rugby Club in Surrey. As usual, Diana insisted on competing in the Mothers' race. The previous year, she had come second . . . but this time she was determined to win. Her joy, lifting her arms as she hit the tape, was obvious. Harry was absolutely delighted his mother had won — and rewarded her with a hug.

In March 1991, Diana brought William to Llandaff Cathedral for his first official engagement in Wales. During a pause, she leant over, placed her hand on his shoulder and whispered: "You're doing just fine."

Diana usually had a smile on her face but when she was with her boys you could see how proud she was of them. In 1990 the boys buried her in the sand during a holiday with Diana's mother to Richard Branson's island in the British Virgin Islands. A year later all three got soaked with her as they went on the Maid of the Mist to get a tourist's view of Niagara Falls.

In Lech, Austria, Di and the boys skied all day but on one of the nights she organised a real treat — a horse-drawn sleigh to take the three of them to a special fondue restaurant in the mountains. As the three of them cuddled up under their sheepskin blanket, their giggles and delight were obvious. Diana was like a child again that afternoon — laughing and almost jumping up and down with excitement. Look at William's face — how many times have you seen this boy look this happy?

But the smiles also hid the heartache. In 1987 Charles and Di took a holiday with the boys in Majorca with King Carlos and Queen Sofia of Spain. Diana still managed a smile, and posed with the boys, but behind the scenes the marriage was beginning to fall apart.

Chapter Four

The Princess In Public

Diana began her royal duties with Charles within weeks of returning from their honeymoon when they went off to the Principality of Wales. Their visit to Haverfordwest was marked by heavy rain and by the end of the day, the feathers on Diana's hat had wilted. But she was not phased — she just got on with the job. She turned down offers of a raincoat as she felt the public wanted to see her, not for her to be hidden away under a mackintosh.

Not surprisingly, Diana was an instant smash. The people of Wales were the first to take her to their hearts. Although she appeared nervous and shy it helped her face her first public ordeal. She was immediately dubbed 'Shy-Di'. Diana said that no one had told her what to do. No one from the royal family, nor their aides, had explained how a Princess should behave. She just went out there and acted naturally. Her forte was small talk — especially with children and older people. Di-mania was well and truly underway. Diana became a star who was quickly to outshine her husband — and he was not used to it. In the days before he met Diana, Charles had been used to getting all the attention. But he got a sharp lesson: he was no longer the main attraction. During one visit, crowds lined either side of the street and Charles and Di split up to

work both sides. The side that got Charles would groan in dismay. He tried to make light of it and told them: "Sorry, you have got me. You better ask for your money back." On another occasion when the moaning continued he told them: "I'll have to split Diana in half so that she can walk down both sides of the street at the same time." Not only was Britain gripped by Di-mania, Australia and New Zealand followed suit, and then Canada. Her early public duties followed the usual royal route of cutting ribbons and opening events, but soon her popularity in meeting people overtook everything else. Her remarkable personal warmth as a comforter of the sick, needy and dying was soon clear to everyone. Against advice from Buckingham Palace, Diana adopted the cause of Aids victims, doing much to dispel the common belief of the times that social contact — even shaking hands — could spread the disease. In later years with the same compassion, she helped to dispel myths about Leprosy. Diana was fast becoming the People's Princess.

There have been many highlights throughout Diana's extraordinary life that helped turn her into a legend. One such night came in December 1985 when she and Charles attended a charity evening together at the Royal Opera House in London's Covent Garden. Charles was in for one of the

biggest surprises of his life as he took his seat with Diana. Unbeknown to him Diana had been secretly practising with diminutive dancer Wayne Sleep. She disappeared from Charles' side and minutes later she astonished him and other guests when she appeared on stage in a daring, low-cut skimpy cream gown standing next to 5ft 2in Wayne. They put on a sensational three-minute act which drew gasps of admiration and disbelief from the audience. Wayne hoisted Di, who stands at 5ft 10in, above his head again and again. The dazzling dance was a show-stopper. At the end of the performance Diana politely curtsied to Prince Charles and he, like everyone in the audience, stood to roar their approval.

However, what no one knew then was that behind the scenes, the royal marriage was already beginning to show signs of strain, and Diana had arranged the sensational surprise performance as a special Christmas present to her husband as a way to help save their marriage.

Diana attended her last Garter Ceremony at Windsor Castle with Charles in June 1992. As they sat in the carriage together, the signs of strain were clear — just a few months later they separated.

Diana was unhappy the whole afternoon and it was obvious that the last place she wanted to be was in a carriage with Charles.

The thing Diana loved about going to Royal Ascot was getting dressed up — and I loved going to Ascot just to photograph her. She would arrive in an open-top carriage with a different member of the royal family each day. I never photographed her sitting next to the Prince at the event, because protocol dictated that he had to sit with the Queen, Prince Philip and the principal guest in the first carriage.

I am sure Princess Alexandra and the Queen Mother will look back on those wonderful summer days and remember Diana's laughter and joy as the crowds shouted her name.

This was one of the rewards for Prince Charles when his team won a polo match — he got kisses from the Mrs. Whether it was at Windsor, in Adelaide or America, we knew that if Diana was presenting the prize, we would get a front page picture.

During a visit to a Merseyside Housing project in November 1995, cyclist Paul Fahy grabbed the headlines when he stole a kiss from the Princess. He was on his way home when he saw Diana walking down the street with civic dignitaries. He stopped and said: "Hi Di, can I have a kiss." Di turned and said: "Come on then, what are you waiting for."

Our nickname for Diana was 'Blue Eyes', and no other person I know has that same sparkling look. She was always a beautiful woman, but her eyes were one of her most outstanding features. Sometimes happy, sometimes sad, sometimes weepy, but always the part of her picture I looked at first. She could always melt the coldest heart with one look.

One of Diana's passions was supporting young ballet dancers. She herself confessed that she would have liked to have been a ballet dancer but lamented that she grew too tall. In this picture I took in 1995, she made one of her visits to a ballet school to watch a practice session.

Diana was pleased as punch to be Colonel-in-Chief of the then Royal Hampshire Regiment and she wore their badge with pride. The Regiment — now renamed the Princess of Wales Royal Regiment — had their cap badge made into a diamond brooch and she wore it every time she attended any of their parades.

Diana represented the Queen at the Sovereign's parade at
Sandhurst. For a second, while she was reviewing the
troops, she was standing in line with the officer cadets.
One frame was all I needed to get this picture. It's one of
my favourites.

In June 1994 Diana took part in the
50th anniversary commemorations of the
D-Day landings. In Portsmouth, she looked
stunning while she chatted to Princess Anne's
husband Captain Tim Laurence.

Diana always looked a million dollars but she was always her most stylish on evening engagements.

The way she mixed the dresses with her jewellery was always elegant. She very seldom got it wrong.

Diana had one quality that no other member of the royal family possesses — she had street cred. She felt at ease with kings and presidents as well as the disadvantaged, the unemployed and the ordinary man and woman on the street. When jobless Danny Walters reached out from the crowd during Di's visit to Southwark, London, he just said to her: "Gimme five." Di happily responded with a friendly slap.

But Danny was able to give Di a more traditional greeting — he kissed her hand and gave her a bunch of flowers, and became another member of the huge army of people who fell in love with the People's Princess. Diana never ignored the people who came to see her and rewarded long waits with a lengthy walkabout. Although the Queen did the first ever royal walkabout, it was Diana who made it her own.

Chapter Five

A Princess To The World

Diana became a global ambassador for Britain with the many tours she made throughout the world. There is hardly one corner of the world Diana did not visit during her tragically short life. As a result of those visits, British business boomed around the world and, of course, the many charities she supported also benefited. In 1985 she joined Charles on a trip to the US, where they attended a VIP dinner at the White House thrown by the then president Ronald Reagan and his First Lady Nancy. Movie heart-throb John Travolta moved forward and asked the Princess on to the dance floor. They thrilled the world to fever pitch. Every twirl at the glittering charity night in Washington raised thousands for charity. Despite living in the heady world of showbusiness Travolta was left captivated by the Princess. He said after: "For 15 lovely minutes, she made me feel like a prince. It was absolutely magical." For Diana, the world had now become her stage.

She had seen the survivors among the poor street children of Rio de Janeiro, Brazil, whose lives were labelled worthless by the wealthy, who believed their businesses were being affected. Diana also visited Mother Teresa's base in Calcutta, another place where human life can seem to be worth little. She tore down barriers and taboos as no one had done before. On a trip to Nigeria, the Princess unhesitatingly held hands with lepers, sat on their beds and played board games with them. And as she had done with Aids, she helped remove the stigma attached to these appalling diseases. In Pakistan, she cradled a dying boy — the pictures were favourites of hers because she felt they represented her humanitarian calling.

In war-torn Sarajevo — her last foreign tour — she again displayed her human touch when she consoled a mother who had come to lay flowers on the grave of her son killed in Bosnia. Diana was never overshadowed by world leaders and often as a result of meeting Diana, they gained popularity in their own countries. One such leader was Portuguese president Marioa Soares in 1987. Diana amazed guests when she twanged his braces and flirted with him, saying: "If I get cold, will you warm me up?" In May 1990, on a visit to Hungary, Diana comforted the country's new First Lady when she burst into tears. Mrs Szuza Goncz, wife of Hungary's first non-Communist president for 43 years, wept unashamedly as she met Charles and Di at the start of a royal visit. Diana gently held her by the hand and continued to hold on until they reached the waiting cars.

In Japan she delighted her hosts with a speech in Japanese at a visit to a children's hospital. She took lessons in London, and the Japanese took her to their hearts because she had taken the time and effort to learn just a few words.

In February 1992, Diana and Charles visited India and the signs of hostility between the Wales' were there for all to see. Charles stayed behind to address businessmen — a decision he later admitted was a mistake — while Diana went to visit love's greatest monument, the Taj Mahal. She sat all alone, looking forlorn. Just a few days later, on the eve of St Valentine's day, Diana made her point clear at a polo match in Jaipur. When Charles went to kiss her, she turned her head away and he ended up brushing her ear. We all knew the fairytale was coming to an end. A few months later the couple made their last official tour together to Korea. They were clearly miserable with each other and their cheerless faces earned them the nickname 'The Glums'. They both let Britain down on that day. Within a few weeks of returning to Britain they announced their separation.

In 1983 Charles and Diana set off to tour Australia. It was dubbed the 'love tour' and these pictures tell you why. They gave each other long, lustful looks — there was obviously a strong bond between them.

This photograph (above) captured all their emotions at once. One afternoon, in stifling 100-degree heat, I followed the couple to a jamboree in Maitland, New South Wales. Then came this extraordinary moment — Charles placed a protective hand on Diana's wrist and whispered: "You're doing a great job." She leaned towards him and replied with a smile of pure gratitude and joy.

Diana went out to see troops in July 1993 and took soldier-mad young Harry with her. Harry was dressed up with Di to review the troops, but he soon got into a specially-made army uniform and was allowed a trip in a real tank.

The last picture of Diana on a foreign tour. She was just about to leave Bosnia in August 1997 when the French Colonel in charge of these troops asked her to pose with his lads. As usual, Diana obliged.

Overleaf: *Diana eased the worries of service wives and families during the Gulf War in February 1991, when she flew in for a visit. She walked among them, chatted and laughed, and shared their worries and fears. This photograph shows Diana in a sea of red, white and blue, and sums up the incredible depth of feeling that women and children alike, from all around the world, had for her.*

On the 'love tour' of Australia in 1983, Charles and Diana had the chance for a bit of sightseeing.
At Ayers Rock, Diana skipped across the hard stone of one of the most famous tourist spots in the world.

One of the moments that touched Princess Diana most was a visit to Mother Teresa's order, the Missionaries of Charity in Calcutta. Although Mother Teresa was in America at the time, recovering from an illness, Diana could clearly see her influence in helping the poor of India. The nuns sang for the Princess, and she had a tear in her eye as she left.

On their tour of Brazil in April 1991, Charles and Di stopped en route to pose together. They were both wearing sunglasses and refused to take them off. We all knew by then that although they were both smiling, there was sadness behind their dark glasses.

In March 1992, Diana showed how warm she was when she gripped this lady's hand with both hers. It was a friendly, comforting gesture, typical of a Princess who instantly made people feel at ease. She made everyone, including this charity worker, feel on top of the world.

During their Brazil tour, Diana went on a school visit and was due to be taken around by officials. But instead of a stiff, formal tour, she reached out and took this girl's hand — and didn't let go for an hour.

When Di attended the enthronement of the new Emperor of Japan, I was the only non-Asian photographer around at the end of the party: "Ma'am, Ma'am, I need a good picture." As she turned to Prince Albert I got this picture.

I took this picture during Diana's visit to Saudi Arabia. Di was only the second woman — apart from his wives and a Saudi astronaut — to be privately entertained by King Fahd.

The last tour Charles and Diana made together was in Korea in November 1992. From the moment they arrived, misery was written all over their faces. I took this picture as they visited a memorial site. The extent of their mutual loathing hit me like a brick. This picture told the world that there was no love left and my heart went out to her. It was dubbed 'The Tour of the Glums'.

The top picture will haunt Prince Charles forever — the day in March 1992 when he preferred to address a group of businessmen in New Delhi while Diana sat all alone at the greatest monument to love, the Taj Mahal. Even Charles admitted later he had made a mistake. Diana described it as a "healing experience." She was also happy to pose for me to give me this exclusive shot.

Diana decided to pursue her role as an unofficial global ambassador for Britain when she made visits to Zimbabwe, India and Pakistan. All these visits came after her split from Charles. It is ironic to think now that Government plans were underway when she died, to make her an official ambassador to represent Britain — there would have been none better.

Chapter Six

The Queen Of Hearts

Diana announced in her devastating *Panorama* interview in 1995: "I would like to be the Queen of people's hearts." Her greatest gift was the deep love she felt for ordinary people — particularly those who were in some way disadvantaged. One of the many tragedies of her death is that the working Princess had already made plans to continue her work.

She had been planning to visit an Aids hospital in Thailand later in 1997, where her presence would have revitalised efforts to find a vaccine which could protect us in the future. It is very difficult to think of anyone else who could make such a difference. She had also been preparing to join forces with South African president, Nelson Mandela, for a new international campaign on behalf of Aids sufferers. And the Leprosy Mission, too, was due to discuss with Diana a proposed tour to Bangladesh for 1998. She made her ambition clear on a hospital visit in London when she announced: "Anywhere I see suffering is where I want to be, doing what I can."

Her latest cause — spearheading the campaign to ban landmines worldwide — was gathering momentum. It was a subject she felt deeply and passionately about, and she had promised to do more to help. Americans Ken Rutherford and Jerry White, themselves victims of landmines, took her on her last foreign trip in July 1997. She had already made a visit to Angola for the same cause,

but on this trip she saw the work being done in war-ravaged Bosnia. Ken Rutherford summed up the feelings of many other charity workers: "She took two obscure Americans under her wing and projected us on the world stage because she took up our cause.

"She promised to continue to support us, and all the victims whom she met in Bosnia felt for the first time they had at long last found a voice for them. A lot of politicians talked and talked about these dreadful weapons, but the Princess did more than talk. She acted and her actions had statesmen throughout the world listening. She gave us heart to go on. She was the driving force by her sheer inspiration and encouragement." Diana's earlier trip to Angola was also ground-breaking. When she walked courageously through a minefield she underlined the importance of her humanitarian work. It will remain one of her lasting legacies. In 1995 her work was officially recognised when the United Cerebral Palsy Foundation presented her with the Humanitarian of the Year Award.

Diana herself once complained that she wanted to be seen as a "work-horse and not as a clothes-horse" after comment was made on one of her outfits. But it was through fashion that the Princess was able to help others. She knew she had pulling power and wherever Diana turned up, the jet set turned out to spend money like it was going out of

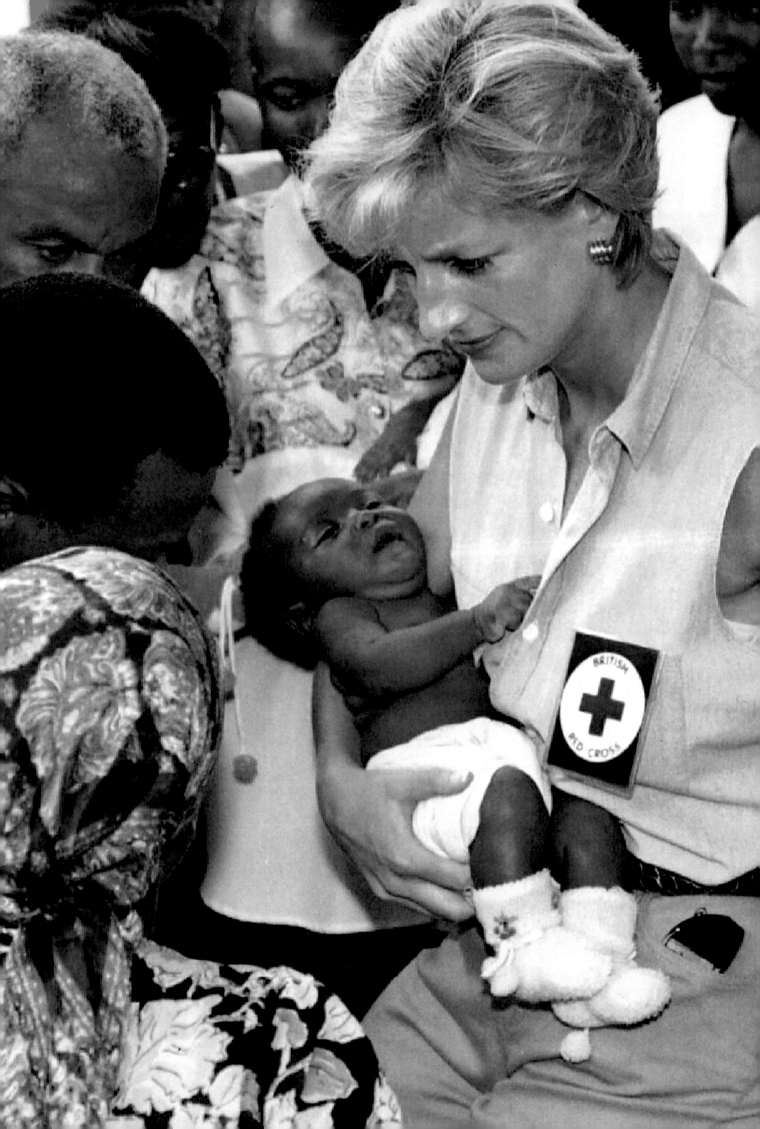

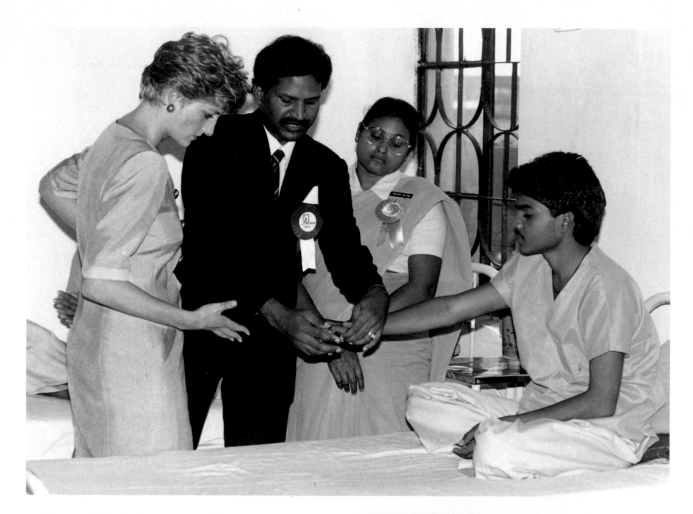

style. Needy kids from Barnardo's benefited to the tune of £300,000 in just one night from a charity event in London in 1985. Mike Whitlam, from the British Red Cross, summed it up simply: "She helped make the world a better place. She would give people who felt they had no hope, the hope they so desperately craved." Her own 36th birthday on 1 July was not spent enjoying herself but out at a fundraising dinner to mark the centenary of London's Tate Gallery.

Just a few days earlier, in June 1997, the Princess helped raise more than £2 million when the auction house Christies put 79 of her dresses up for sale in New York. Her 'going, going, Gown' show helped two of her favourite charities — the Royal Marsden Hospital cancer fund and the Aids Crisis Trust. Her own son William came up with the idea of auctioning off the dresses she no longer wore. William's brainwave was a clear indication that the lessons Diana had taught her son about helping others were already beginning to take root. The dress that raised the most, lot 79, which Diana wore when she danced with Hollywood star, John Travolta, sold for £120,301.

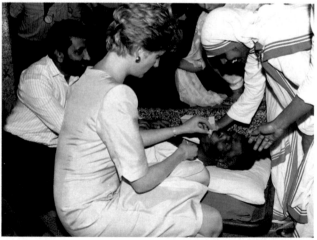

Diana was always a hands-on Princess. One touch from her gave so much comfort. At Mother Teresa's Hospice in Calcutta, Diana spent two hours visiting every patient in an overcrowded room, bringing some solace in their last few moments.

Diana helped remove some of the stigma from Aids when she embraced sufferers in Harlem and Brazil. She never flinched. She changed the way I thought and altered the shameful prejudices I once held.
Overleaf: *In 1991, Diana took US First Lady, Barbara Bush, to visit the Aids ward at London's Middlesex Hospital. Diana was deep in conversation with a patient who was in the last stages of the illness. I was so captivated by the compassion Diana showed, that I forgot to take a picture of Mrs Bush!*

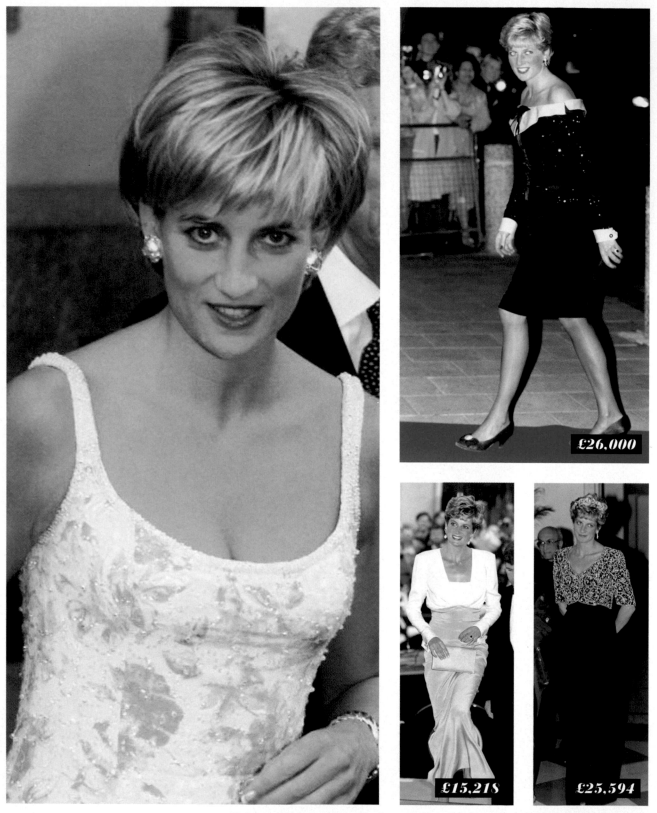

£26,000

£15,218

£25,594

Princess Diana launched one of her biggest charity fundraisers when she put 79 of her own dresses up for sale. Diana attended a special Christies party in New York to launch the sale which raised more than £2 million. All of the money went to her favourite charities, The Royal Marsden cancer fund and the AIDS Crisis Trust. Top bid was £120,301 for Lot 79 — Di's 'Travolta' dress — the one she wore when she danced with the star of Grease at the White House.

Diana had many nights out with the stars, as she continued to help raise funds for Aids sufferers.
Mick Hucknall, George Michael and David Bowie were among those who rallied to help her.

Of all the causes Diana supported, one of her main aims was to help children. Officials and dignitaries were often left kicking their heels while Diana went off to talk to the children. Language was never a barrier — she found it easy to make herself understood. In Bosnia, in August 1997, she met two landmine victims: Serbian Zdravko Beric aged 12 (left) and Malik Bradoric, aged 14, a Muslim. Both boys had lost their legs after stepping onto landmines and they had become friends despite the ethnic differences which had ravaged their country. She left a lasting impression on both boys and Zdravko was brought over by officials of the Landmines Survivors Network to attend her funeral.

She was a woman of a thousand faces who would look beautiful in whatever she wore, and wherever she went. On her Angolan trip in January 1997, Diana donned a protective shield and flak jacket for a tour of a minefield. Diana was determined to get her message across — and taking this risk was a stark reminder to world leaders that she wanted them to listen to the plight of landmine victims.

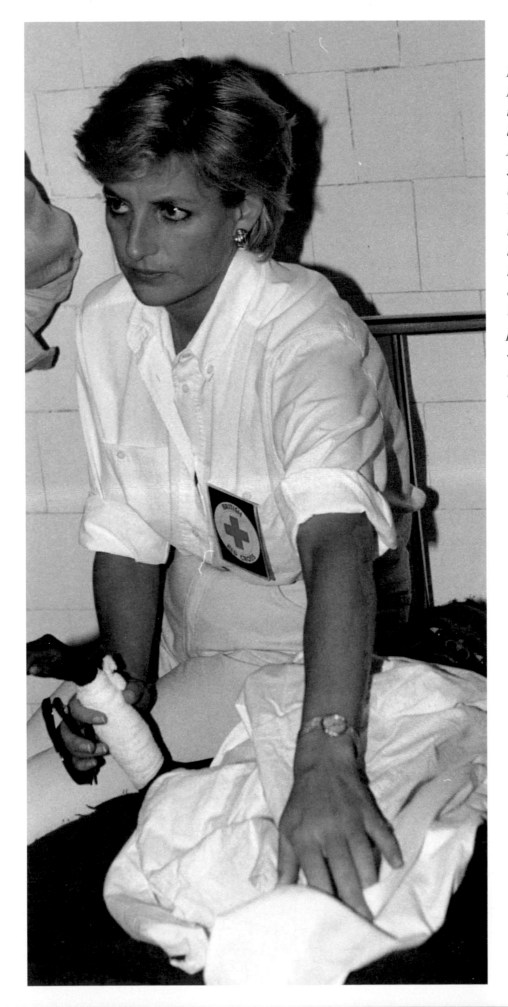

Diana became the People's Princess of the world with her anti-landmines mission. In Angola, I watched her sitting by the hospital bedside of victim Helena Ussova. The Princess held the child's pathetic, stick-like arms. With tears in her eyes, she carefully covered the little girl's body with a sheet to preserve her dignity. She said meeting this girl was the most moving part of her visit. It was for me.

With the Angolan minefield just a few feet away from her, Diana stood next to a warning sign and held a mine made safe by officials from the Halo Trust charity.

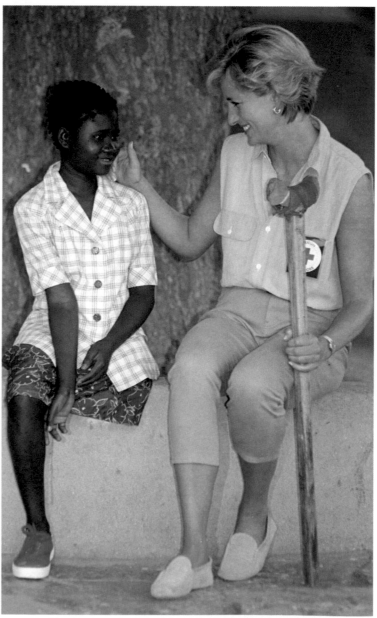

In Angola, Diana sat and chatted to 13-year-old landmine victim Sandra Thijica. Diana gently caressed Sandra's cheek and the Princess gave her one of those famous smiles which tell those in her company that it is they who are special.

The last overseas visit she made was to war-ravaged Bosnia to continue her campaign to ban landmines from the world. In one of the last conversations I had with her she said: "I am not interested in the politicians' criticisms of me, I just want to help these people. I am a humanitarian."

The last portrait I ever took of Diana was in war-torn Bosnia. It was six o'clock in the evening, and she was visiting landmine victims. Dressed casually in an oversized shirt, she could have been going to tea at Buckingham Palace. She looked so beautiful that evening. It was the same natural beauty I first saw when she was a plump, unsure teenager. But she grew into this beautiful, sophisticated woman — and I've never seen beauty quite like it. I don't think I ever will again.

Diana's Charities

The following list identifies the charities which Diana, Princess of Wales continued to support until her death. If you wish to support these charities please contact them directly, or send a cheque or postal order to: The Diana, Princess of Wales Memorial Fund, Kensington Palace, London, W8 4PU

British Red Cross Anti Personnel Land Mines Campaign
Centrepoint (for the young homeless)
The English National Ballet
Great Ormond Street Children's Hospital
The Halo Trust
The Leprosy Mission
The National AIDS Trust
The Royal Marsden Hospital NHS Trust

The following list represents all the charities which Diana, Princess of Wales actively supported until 1996.

The Albany Centre and Theatre ● All England Lawn Tennis & Croquet Club ● American Friends of Covent Garden ● Anglo-European College of Chiropractice ● Association for Spinal Injury Research Rehabilitation & Reintegration Royal National Orthopaedic Hospital ● Douglas Bader Foundation ● Barnardo's ● Benesh Institute of Choreology British Deaf Association ● British Lung Foundation ● British Youth Opera ● Chester Summer Music Festival Chicken Shed Theatre Company ● Child Accident Prevention Trust ● Commonwealth Society for the Deaf Company of Merchant Taylors ● Disability Sport England ● Dystrophic Epidermolysis Bullosa Research Association (Princess Diana VB Memorial Research Fellowship) ● Eureka! The Children's Museum ● Faculty of Dental Surgery of the Royal College of Surgeons of England ● Foundation for Conductive Education ● The Freshfield Service Friends of the Imperial War Museum ● General Council & Registry of Osteopaths ● Headway National Head Injuries Association ● Help the Aged ● Home-Start ● Honourable Society of the Middle Temple ● Huntingdon's Disease Association ● Institute for the Study of Drug Dependents ● International Spinal Research Trust ● David Lloyd Slazenger Racquet Club ● London City Ballet NOW City Ballet of London ● London Symphony Orchestra National Hospital for Neurology & Neurosurgery Development Foundation ● National Meningitis Trust ● Natural History Museum ● Newport International Competition for Young Pianists ● Nothern Ireland Pre-School Playgroups Association ● Parkinson's Disease Society of UK ● Pre-School Learning Alliance ● Printers Charitable Corporation Relate ● Royal Academy of Music ● Royal & Sun Alliance Gloucestershire County Cricket Club ● Royal Anthropological Institute of Great Britain & Ireland ● Royal College of Obstetricians & Gynaecologists ● Royal College of Physicians & Surgeons of Glasgow ● St Mary's Save the Baby Fund ● St Matthew Society ● Sargent Cancer Fund for Children ● Scottish Pre-School Playgroups ● SEEABILITY, The Royal School for the Blind Swansea Festival of Music and Arts ● Trust for Sick Children in Wales ● Turning Point ● Wales Pre-School Playgroups Association ● WellBeing ● Welsh Bowling Association ● Welsh National Opera Ltd ●

Chapter Seven

The Princess At Play

Diana often condemned herself, saying she was as "thick as two short planks." She even said her brain was the size of a pea. But she had a quick mind and could hold her own with the best of them.

And the woman who captured the hearts of millions with her caring and compassion, who captivated everyone she met, often let her hair down when she was free to do so. She loved gossip and giggling at naughty jokes and she was also quick-witted which enabled her to tease friends — and often reporters and photographers too. During one trip to Zimbabwe with the British Red Cross, Diana was taken to a village in the bush which had been given a water supply for the first time, which meant the local people did not have to march barefoot for hours. She was accompanied by Red Cross Director General Mike Whitlam and when they arrived at lunch-time a small queue had started to form — the villagers were waiting for their meal which had been cooked in a communal open-air kitchen. Mike asked the Princess to help serve the porridge-like meal into wooden and metal bowls — and as she picked up the ladle hundreds more villagers suddenly descended to turn the queue into a huge snake-like procession. Diana started to giggle and turned to Mike to tell him: "Now look what you have got me into. If you think I am doing the washing up, you have got another think coming. I think you should do it." She often

combined her humour with her concern and compassion for others. Royal photographer Arthur Edwards experienced it first hand during a trip to Cairo in May 1992. He had caught dysentery and for three days was too ill to leave his bed. As soon as Diana heard that Arthur was ailing, she sent her personal physician — who travelled with her — to his bedside and the next day one of her police bodyguards brought mineral salts to help rehydrate his body. He managed to return to work to photograph her at the Cairo Museum and Diana came over to ask how he was. Arthur told her: "I am fine Ma'am, I just haven't eaten anything for three days." Diana laughed: "Yes I can see that. It has done wonders for your waistline!" On flights home from foreign tours, Diana would often be sitting in the steward's galley, dressed in her track suit with bare feet, inviting members of the press who had been accompanying her to have some fun. "Come and join me, we are having a party," she said.

Some friends were startled to get phone calls and the chirpy voice at the other end announcing: "Hi, it's Disco Di here from KP (Kensington Palace)." Naturally, some of Diana's happiest moments came when she was on holiday with her sons. During an official tour of Canada, she took them on the Maid of the Mist, to get a clear view of Niagara Falls. It was also on that trip that the memory of Diana as a mother was captured in one

single photograph — when she ran forward, arms outstretched, on board the Royal Yacht Britannia to greet William and Harry. She was so pleased to see her boys that she ignored VIPs and other dignitaries to race towards them, and to give them one of her famous hugs.

On one bucket-and-spade holiday in 1990, Diana had taken the boys to Richard Branson's secluded holiday island in the British Virgin Islands. Halfway through the week, the Princess was buried in the sand by her impish sons — another experience she shared with many parents with young boistrous children. The seclusion of the island meant they had a quiet time, but on the last day of the holiday Diana decided she wanted a livelier night and asked for a local band from a nearby island to come over. It was especially memorable for one man — her police bodyguard Inspector Ken Wharfe. He was one of the few men around and so he became her dancing partner for most of the evening.

As well as sunshine holidays the Princess took the youngsters on ski trips and it was in Lech, Austria, that they learned to ski. Harry took to it like a duck to water, but at first William decided he did not like the cold. However, both boys persisted and now they are expert skiers. At the time they left Diana complaining: "They are so good, I cannot keep up with them." In 1994 Diana took the boys white water rafting in Colorado, where they stayed with Goldie Hawn and Kurt Russell, for one of their best ever holidays.

Dancing Queen Diana waltzed onto the dance floor in Melbourne in 1985.
Previous Page: *Diana was always full of surprises and she did not let us down when she arrived for a glittering ball at the Southern Cross Hotel in 1985. I knew she would be wearing a new ballgown, and I hoped the outfit would be sensational enough to make a front page picture. Her hair was fantastic — she looked every inch a supermodel. I had my front page photograph, and I learned from that day on never to take Diana for granted.*

*Three years later she was dancing with Prince Charles again.
It was the only time she and Charles ever let the press see them
waltz. She looked truly sensational — and she knew it.*

Diana went on her first ski trip with Prince Charles to his favourite resort of Klosters, Switzerland, in 1987. A year later tragedy struck when a close friend of the couple, Major Hugh Lindsay, was killed in an avalanche. Charles narrowly escaped death but another close friend, Patty Palmer-Tomkinson, was badly injured. Diana vowed never to return and later went with her sons to Lech, in Austria where the boys learned to ski.

I have taken many photographs of the Princess of Wales, but these two, left & below — separated by almost seven years — are among my favourites. In 1990 she went on a bucket-and-spade holiday to Richard Branson's island in the British Virgin Islands and wore a dynamite leopardskin swimsuit on the beach — she could put any supermodel to shame. In the summer of 1997, Diana cooled off under the sweltering heat with a swim in the Mediterranean. It was her last holiday with the boys — and this is one of the last pictures I ever took of Diana.

Chapter Eight

A Princess Of Fashion

Diana turned up to the Serpentine Galley on a summer's evening in June 1994 in a dress she only decided to wear at the last minute. It was a decision which blew her estranged husband off the front pages. Earlier that day he had admitted his adultery on television. Diana had been due to wear a dress made for her by Gianni Versace, but instead she wore a sexy off-the-shoulder outfit by Christina Stambolian. Diana's dazzling beauty and radiant smile made her an ideal cover girl and in the same way she was a profile-raiser for charity, she was an inspiration to the fashion world.

On formal occasions she drew gasps of admiration with whatever she wore. Indeed, Diana is largely credited with helping to boost the profits of the British fashion industry single-handedly. Her sexy outfits and style achieved her ultimate aim — to help promote the cause or charity she was supporting. Diana once cheekily complained: "When I wear a backless dress, I find that most people just don't know where to put their hands." At first, designers were instructed to make evening dresses with high necks which in some way reflected her caution. Much later she wanted to show off her figure with more confidence. She trained and worked out regularly, first at the Chelsea Harbour gym and later at the

Earls Court gym. She was also a keen swimmer. Magazine editors all over the world replaced the highest paid models with Diana because they could not match up to her star quality and international appeal. But Diana looked natural and relaxed even wearing a plain black jumper and leggings. One of the most memorable fashion shoots she undertook was in 1992 for photographer Patrick Demarchelier, and his pictures appeared in the top fashion magazine *Vogue*. She was a *Vogue* cover girl two years later in 1994. That time the proceeds from the shoot went to two of her favourite charities — DEBRA, an organisation for people with skin diseases, and the Chicken Shed Theatre Company, which helps disadvantaged and handicapped children. Just two months before she died, Diana appeared at her most fresh and sexy for *Vanity Fair*. The series of poses for photographer Mario Testino clearly showed the sparkle had returned as she had come to terms with her new life as a divorced woman. But she was as much at home in a couture ball gown as she was in her gym kit or with windswept hair and a bullet-proof waistcoat on the minefields of Angola.

She inspired many other women to dress like her. Since her wedding day, other brides around the world imitated her. When she slicked her hair back,

so did they. When she hid her eyes under her fringe, they too copied her. In the main she supported British designers, like Zandra Rhodes, Elizabeth Emanuel, Bruce Oldfield and Catherine Walker. But she also had soft spots for Jacques Azagury and John Galliano, and of course for the late Gianni Versace.

She was continually included on every "best dressed" list worth mentioning — which helped designers command high fees for their creations.

Tall, slim and graceful Diana could carry off whatever she wore, and over the years she dramatically changed her style time and again. Since the early days of her marriage to Charles, Diana evolved from a fresh faced Sloane into a stunningly sophisticated beauty. It was in the nineties that she honed her style to perfection with a breathtaking parade of figure-hugging evening gowns. But no matter what outfit she wore, the warm woman underneath shone through.

Diana always turned it on for the big nights out. The traffic stopped and the flashbulbs popped. Whether it was at the Cannes Film Festival or around town in London, Diana was a showstopper.

Facing Page: *A completely relaxed and informal shot of Diana at a polo game in 1985 — one of my all time favourites. She was having a bad hair day, so donned a headscarf instead. She dodged the camera because she thought she looked terrible — but everyone was transfixed by her natural beauty. And whether she was in Southall, London or Lahore, Pakistan, the Princess always made sure her head was respectfully covered when she visited mosques.*

Diana took flower power to heady new heights. She could never go anywhere without someone wanting to give her a bunch. Often after her hospital visits she would be laden down with bouquets. Diana herself would certainly have appreciated the millions of flowers that were laid outside royal palaces following her death — particularly at Kensington Palace. The ocean of flowers outside her former home will always remain one of the most vivid memories of the whole tragedy.

Diana was always a Pearly Queen. She loved her pearls, especially the chokers which she used to great effect. A golden light fell gently on the face of a golden lady in Buenos Aires in December 1995. Dressed in white with a magnificent pearl set, Diana looked like an angel. She also looked stunning at a charity lunch in Sydney (far right).

I chose this beautiful portrait for one important reason — it was Diana's last engagement as Her Royal Highness, before the title was so cruelly stripped from her. Attending a dinner at Chicago in November 1996, she dazzled and shone. Everything — her hair, her eyes, the make-up — was perfect.

One of the most memorable occasions came in June 1994, on the day that Prince Charles admitted his adultery on TV. Diana was due for an engagement at the Serpentine Gallery in London's Hyde Park. I had been waiting at least ten hours for her to turn up to make sure I had a front position ahead of all the other photographers. But the wait was worthwhile — the sun had just set, the evening light was golden, and Diana glowed. Her whole face and body lit up, and the incredible sequence was like a slow-motion scene from a Hollywood movie. Fifteen minutes before Diana arrived, Versace released a press statement saying she was due to wear one of his creations. When she arrived, she leapt out of the car and ran towards the waiting officials. The beautiful, off-the-shoulder, sexy black dress took our breath away, and we all wrote about the stunning Versace gown. It was only later we discovered the truth. Just ten minutes before she set off, Diana had a sudden change of heart about her outfit. She discarded her Versace dress and chose an incredible number by Christina Stambolian instead. In a matter of minutes, she had hastily pulled together a completely new look. It blew Charles straight off the front pages. HE was the story — SHE was the picture.

Chapter Nine

A Princess Remembered

Diana was honoured with a state funeral — in all but name. It was a unique funeral for a unique person. The public outpouring of grief was extraordinary as the people said farewell to their Princess. There are many aspects of the day that will be forever etched in people's memories — the shattering of tradition with the Union Jack flying at half-mast on top of Buckingham Palace; the strength Prince William and Prince Harry mustered to walk with their father, Prince Charles, uncle Earl Spencer and grandfather Prince Philip behind the coffin to Westminster Abbey. Propped up on one of the wreaths on top of her coffin was a card bearing one heart-breaking word: 'Mummy' — Prince Harry's personal tribute to his mother.

More than one million people lined the streets of the funeral route. Many, many more lined the 77-mile route to Althorp, her family home and final resting place. The scenes of people standing on the M1 motorway, lovingly throwing flowers as the hearse passed by is another lasting image. Just as Diana had shattered traditions throughout her life, traditions fell at her funeral. Elton John sang his new version of *Candle in the Wind*, specially adapted in honour of our 'English rose'. The Earl Spencer gave a moving tribute to his sister when he said of her: "We give thanks for the life of a woman I am so proud to call my sister, the unique, the complex, the extraordinary and irreplaceable Diana, whose beauty, both internal and external will never be extinguished from our minds."

The applause from the streets — muffled to those in the Abbey — grew and grew until it swept inside. The 2,000 mourners took it up until the whole Abbey reverberated. A single golden sunbeam came through the window high in the vaulted nave and lit up Diana's coffin. Outside the Abbey, Arthur Edwards stood waiting as the funeral procession paused briefly for a one-minute silence. Arthur remembers: "All I could hear around me was the sobbing of women, men and children. It was the most moving sound I have ever heard.

"Diana gave me the best pictures anybody could ever take. She took me to places in the world I never thought I would ever go. She treated me — the cockney son of a lorry driver — as an equal, despite her aristocratic background. She called me by my first name, she even teased me about my weight and my bald patch — and she always made me laugh. But more than anything, I saw in her kindness and compassion for other people. Through her actions, she showed me the way to behave. And like the rest of the world, I learned from her magnificent example. That is what has been so cruelly taken away from us. The Princess who shone is no longer here to sparkle — to light up our lives. I loved her. You all loved her. She will always be our Princess."

This is the photograph I never dreamed in a million years that I would ever take. For 17 wonderful years, Diana had been a huge part of my life. When I landed in Paris at 5am and was told in a brief, terrible phone call that Diana was dead, I didn't want to believe it. I was choking back the tears as I took this picture. As the coffin was put into the hearse, I watched Diana's sisters help each other to the car. I left the hospital feeling that the saddest job of my life had just been completed.

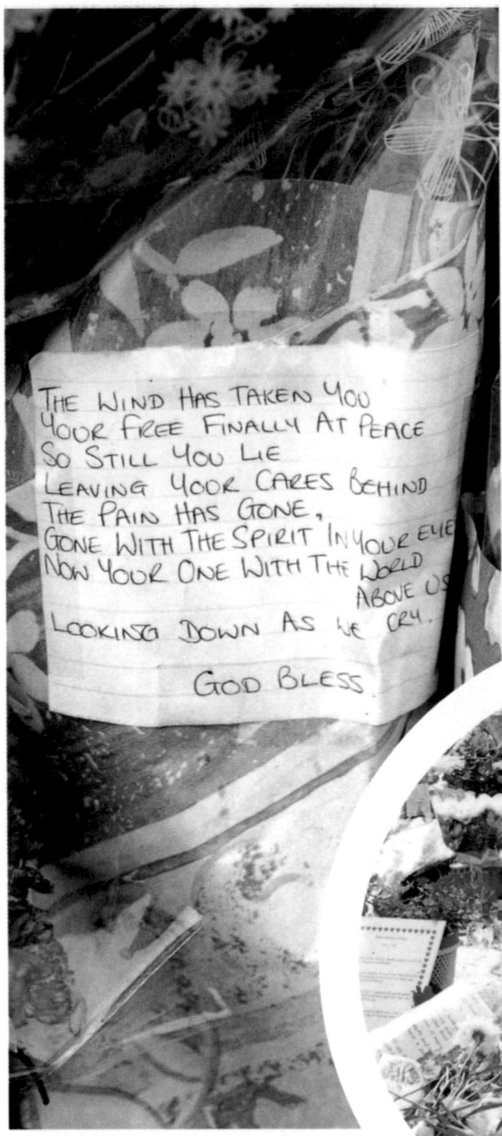

THE WIND HAS TAKEN YOU
YOUR FREE FINALLY AT PEACE
SO STILL YOU LIE
LEAVING YOOR CARES BEHIND
THE PAIN HAS GONE,
GONE WITH THE SPIRIT IN YOUR EYE
NOW YOUR ONE WITH THE WORLD
                    ABOVE US
LOOKING DOWN AS WE CRY.

GOD BLESS.

Diana, ——
You were our Shining Light, ——
the World is now a darker
place.
In our hearts and minds
    forever,
        With love
            Debbie xx

Dearest
William & HARRY
With MUCH LOVE!

MOTHERS Never
really DIE, They
JUST Keep HOUSE
UP IN THE SKY.
THEY PoLiSH The SUN
By day & Light the
TWINKLING STARS That
Shine At Night
and in heavenly home
ABovE They Wait to
Welcome Those
They LoVE!

Thinking of you Both
you Were Very Lucky to
of had Such a Wonderful
Mother Never To Be
forgotten
        Love NICOLA
            Thorpe

We miss you Diana.

LOVE Nicky S
age 7

Diana's final resting place.

*"Nothing brings me more happiness than trying
to help the most vulnerable people in society.
If anyone in distress calls, I will rush to them
wherever I am. I touch people — it is a gesture,
which comes naturally to me from the heart."*

Diana, Princess of Wales — August 1997